Grace Nichols was born and educated in Guyana, a former British South American colony. She moved to Britain in 1977 and since then has had many books published for both adults and children. Her first book of poems, *I Is A Long-Memoried Woman*, won the 1983 Commonwealth Poetry Prize. Virago published her other collections: *The Fat Black Woman's Poems* (1984), *Lazy Thoughts of A Lazy Woman* (1989), *Sunris* (1996), winner of the Guyana Poetry Prize, and her first novel, *Whole of A Morning Sky* (1986).

Her books for children include two collections of short stories and several books of poems. *Paint Me A Poem* (2004) won the Children's Poetry Best Single Author Collection. She has also edited a number of children's anthologies including *From Mouth to Mouth* (2004), which she co-edited with her partner, the poet John Agard.

She spends her time writing as well as travelling around the country reading to GCSE students who study her work. She served as poet-in-residence at the National Institute of Education, University of Singapore; University of the West Indies, Cave Hill, Barbados and at the Tate Gallery, London, 1999–2000.

Her awards include a Cholmondeley Award, a CLPE Award and an Honorary Degree from the Open University. Grace Nichols has two daughters and lives in Sussex.

Also by Grace Nichols

GRACE NICHOLS
Startling
THE
FLYING FISH

Virago

VIRAGO

First published in Great Britain in December 2005 by Virago Press

Copyright © Grace Nichols 2005

The moral right of the author has been asserted.

A CIP catalogue record for this book
is available from the British Library

ISBN 1 84408 291 1

Typeset in Baskerville by M Rules
Printed and bound in Great Britain by Clays Ltd, St Ives plc

Virago Press
An imprint of
Time Warner Book Group UK
Brettenham House
Lancaster Place
London WC2E 7EN

www.virago.co.uk

To the memory of my mother who stayed

And to those overseas who still
carry the Cariwoma spirit

Special thanks are due to the following authors and the books that I found informative and stimulating while working on *Startling the Flying Fish*.

Memory of Fire by Eduardo Galeano (translated by Cedric Belfrage); *Malinche's Conquest* by Anna Lanyon; *The Popul Vuh: the Quiche Mayan Book of Creation* (translated by Dennis Tedlock); *The Sun and the Drum: African Roots in Jamaican Folk Tradition* by Leonard E. Barrett; *Scattering of Jade* by D.T. J Knab and T. Sullivan (for the Aztec Prayer); *Salt* by Earl Lovelace; *Witch Broom* by Lawrence Scott and *The Dark Jester* by Wilson Harris.

Thanks also to Sebastião Salgado for his exhibition 'Migrations', a photograph from which inspired the poem 'The children of Las Margaritas' (commissioned by the Barbican).

And to Derek Walcott for his epic evocations of the Sea ('the sea is history').

Contents

Three

Four

Five

Be it jade, it shatters.
Be it gold, it breaks.
Be it a quetzal feather, it tears apart.
Not forever on earth; only a little while here.

Aztec Prayer

One

And I Cariwoma
watch my children
take off like
migrating spider-birds
carrying the silver threads
of their linkages,
making of me new
triangulars across Atlantic,
enmeshing me into
their metropolitan affairs –
A thought for one here.
A sigh for one there.
A pride for one somewhere.
Europe? North America?
Smiles at photos
of grands and greatgrands
I've never seen,
the children who shine
like constellations
in my dreams.
For them all I must keep green.
My children are movers.

Yet, each decade
something in them
is lost to us.
Something in them
is gained to their places
of adoption.
Life unravels itself
enough to send them home
on a shoestring,
to whine about
streams dried-up
and horizons too narrow
for their eyes' new circumspect.
Astonished to find
children still swimming
like the little porpoises
they once were –
in the irretrievable rivers
of their childhood.

See our sister – a haunter of beaches
wearing her dress like a symbol?
Staring out to sea and across
the treacherous Atlantic
to where her dreams lie in Miami.
Hear this trapped Persephone, perfumed
with the reckless arrogance of youth:

'I will have my eternal summer of plenty.
I will leave these islands, this underworld
that would crown me *Queen of Poverty*
I will board that unseaworthy boat
matchboxed to a group I hardly know,
except they share my dreams of an El Dorado –
No twinkling Arawak gold this time,
just a piece of life, upward and bright.'

And who has the heart to tell her
she'll find no flowers in neon?
Who has the heart to tell her

that when she least expects it
her own backyard will swim
like a sea beside her?
That she won't escape the voices,
the nuances – much like her mother's blood.

Those farewell party nights.
Watching them dance the dark
into broad daylight.
Watching them disappear
one by one, like stars
into their distant lives.
I can still remember the blushing
black of my Vasti's eyes,
an aspiring tenor getting up
to sing her a fitting
going-to-England tribute –
A room full of dark-eyed girls
glowing in their prime.
In a voice tingling spines,
he sings: Pretty Blue Eyes.

And they all clap loudly
innocent of irony as he.
Innocent of the need of starapples
and sapodillas, all bursting
for one shining glance.

The distant tributaries of my blood.
The tribe that once took succour
in staying together
is now scattered fourways
on the handkerchief of the wind.
And long before the phone
goes dead in its socket
the voice of a beloved
stays warm yet still stranded
from the shore of my skin.

Deep
I Cariwoma
have always
carried deep
these islands,
this piece
of Atlantic coastland
inside me.
Sky-deep
Sea-deep
As star is to stone
As tide is to shore
Is just so I hold
these islands
to my coral bones.
And long before
hurricane strike,
some little butterfly,
some little blue messenger
of the soul, will ride
the wind to bring
first news to my door.

Wind and Shore are my close companions
In my sea-house there are many mansions
Who knows more than me
the songs of the drowning?

Through the artifacts of my shells
I whisper to the living
To the dead I offer a treatise
of continuous remembering –

My memorials between rocks
My altar-places between weeds
Nightly I dance with my children
in the dancehalls of the deep

Yes, I Cariwoma watched history happen
like a two-headed Janus,
however far apart heads can be.

The first head rose up
from the hammock's languorous belly
and turned towards the winged ships
of Columbus's faith,
his bright dreams which soon turned
for us into nightmares.

The other head rose up
from the misery ship, that other hammock,
and swivelled back, locking
as in the deformity of a duenne's foot.
Face as faceless as a duenne,
those bewildered little souls
gazing back in limbo
at the shards of broken pots,
the waves of palmwine betrayal

Only the eyes of the sea-almonds
kept on beckoning –
A cautious welcome across new shores.

But there were other ships
rocked by dreams
and fears and promise

Rolling
with new arrivals
across Atlantic.

From the fields
of Bengal
and Uttar Pradesh,
From Kowloon
and Canton.
From Madeira
and Ireland –

Their indentured mud-
stained feet, soon embroidered
like the slave's instep to the fields.

Their songs of exile
their drums of loss
all caught in a weaving odyssey

of no return.
No waiting Penelope
unpicking all her work.

Two

Islands
Islands
their palm-tree seductions

Pulling tourists like migratory birds –
dwell a moment on these two
women basking on beach-warmth.

One (now in the mid-winter of her life)
claims her husband says
she is no oil painting.

Here with the wide sea, darling,
you can be a dolphin
or newly washed Aphrodite.

And why shouldn't she?
This woman whose red hands
tell their own story.

First-time-Abroad
from England-North,
soak up yourselves

in sunshine and seawater
that will not make you shiver.
No need to know that sea
does not always keep up
this front of blue serenity.

Sitting on the ark of a balcony
facing Atlantic
ocean-spray a heady overture of kisses

Well this is a classic –
the pauses and crashes
the biblical rises

While I like some Mrs Noah stay riveted
trying to still the exuberant waves in me
the movements of pure panic.

Such magnificence will pull something,
and takes it
in the shape of a Canadian tourist

A young male
heading in
despite our crescendo of warning

Surfacing much later on the box

his ecstasy zipped up
his body-bag lifted off

Another life – another unreturning dove.

The *Pinta*
The *Nina*
The *Santa Maria*

The father son and holy ghost
coming across the water –

Three billowing ships
full of adventurers and seasoned sailors
all scrambling around the decks
like mutinous spiders.
All held in check, after three sea-weeks,
by the webbed faith of a stubborn
red-haired Genoese
staring day-in day-out at the horizon.
To turn back now an act of treason.

The *Pinta*
The *Nina*
The *Santa Maria*
sailing over my tongue's edge in a litany

'Tierra Tierra'
that strangled cry
startling the flying-fish
and the long sleep of history.

Oceanic voices
rolling through turquoise
to waves of clearness
An invisible life streaming everywhere
just above the grasp of my fingertips –

Is that you Columbus
I discover in a breeze
still startling the flying-fish
in search of the Indies?

Genoa, Spain, Lisbon are but a pale memory
to this nautical-shadow floating above blue scales
But how could I have foreseen the dark vistas and the tears
the seeds of destruction that would flourish in discovery's wake?
Or that the name of Amerigo Vessupucci would be the necklace
to caress the breast of this continent?
I who near doubled the world and opened
a dazzling seam in Europe's dull vein.
but merely went out convinced
that I had pushed into the Orient.

Ah, it seems as if it were only yesterday
that these islands flowered before me
like a fragrant myth or mirage.
The first I fell upon was Guanahani,
an Indian word which I renamed
San Salvador in honour of our Lord –
Now, even these turquoise waters mock my enterprise
with their Carib name.
Yet if I must be claimed by any
let it be (if they would have me) by the people of the Isles
Here rest my sea-weary bones.
Here haunt my sea-going spirit.

Oceanic voices
rolling through turquoise
to waves of clearness –
Voices now harmless as foam

And I Cariwoma
who never speak too ill of the dead
sit listening as the wind
unfurls its scroll
of old names on my breath

Guanahani   of the white sands
Liamuiga   of the fertile earth
Wa-omoni   of the heron bird
Kairi   of the humming bird
Kiskeya   of the mountainplace
Alliouagana of the prickly pear
Madinina   of the flowers
Xaymaca   of wood and water
Iounalao   of the iguana

whose unconquered gaze still bears witness.

And you, Malinche,
Now that the fog of these centuries
has started to lift a little – I see you
coming through the weight of history –
history with its dates and treaties
history with its goodies and baddies.
Come, my sister, and talk to me.

It is said that you betrayed your people.
That you were the traitor-translator,
the one who with the gift of tongues
bore Cortez an empire as well as a son.
But wasn't it foretold in the ancient prophecies –
that the quetzal would lose its wings
in the fall of Tenochtitlan?

I Malinche, have seen many suns
and many moons of sorrow
my footsteps dogged from childhood
by whispers, rumours, shadows
Perhaps if Popocatepetl or Iztaccihuatl
could speak – not the language of smoke –
but the language of words –

they would tell a different story.
Time and the green jaws of the jungle
have put holes in the leaves of my memory.

Malinchista – they say meaning a sell-out
Malinchista, – a word that shadows your name
But how long can we stare into a mirror of blame?
Accept, O prodigal mother of the mestizo –
this marigold flower for the black cloud of your hair.

Still our Cassandra continues
to scream her truth,
each catastrophe coming
through the caul of her vision

Each catastrophe running
the gauntlet of her tongue
only to fall on the walls
of disbelief and disapproval

Helen. A launching of ships.
Greek gifts.
Her sea-resounding voice
picked up by the ears

Of my own middle passage.
My own ships bowing
in prayer across Atlantic.
Her see-far eyes, like mine

Discerning everything –
from those suicidal Carib leaps

down to the soft massacre at Jonestown –
all the bloody reincarnations of history.

Her spirit-shrieks. My global shudders.
Her poor mother: 'For godsake girl,
spare me these endless gloomy prophecies
these visions of crumbling towers.'

The people could fly –
See them rise up, a cloud of locusts
or more a host of scarecrows in suneye?
Wind flapping against their
sunworn dresses and tattered shirt-coats

This brethren who lived a life
of saltless endurance.
No slave-food – saltbeef, saltfish,
to blight their blood or mock the freedom,
the heady helium gathering slowly in their veins.

How closely they guarded their levitational-mystery
How calmly they carried out their earthly duties

And now it's lift-off time –
See them making for the
green open hilltops
with nothing but their faith
and their corncobs?

Hear them singing; One bright morning
when my work is over I will fly away home . . .

The people could fly.

Look! Look, how they coming, Africa!

'Goodbye plantation goodbye'

Three

Today I sing
not of breakaway
                    calypso islands
but of a mainland built for an Amazon –
A reign of vast rivers
sweeping through the kingdom
of a dense and dreaming vegetation
its volatile sap moving
from darkest-green to olive
from emerald to jade
here, in this rainforest,
where giant bromeliads mingle
with giant ferns and legends rise
like mist from waterfalls.

Today I sing of an Andean fortress
O sacred city in the clouds –
Macchu Picchu wrapping itself in shroud
from conquistador-gaze.
When I think on it – the beauty of it
The ancient spirit
of its Intihuatana stone.

Then I am filled with a strange sadness
and a pride
For this place that
I Cariwoma occupy –
This green space where the Caribbean
and Amazon collide.

When I remember my steamy vegetable romance!
In that green-heart forest that needed no music –
Not with the birds for song
Frogs for bass
Howler-monkeys keeping a low base

And the Chachalaka for bush-alarm

When I remember those slow heavy days
that gave way to cool shivery nights
Those misty mornings that never failed
to fever themselves up or leave me
in a fine sweat of blossoms

Woman paddling canoe
or apparition on river?

Moving borderless
like her Bering
crossing ancestors

Slipping by time
and death and we
on beginning water

O Wapishana
Macusi
Warrau

All your tribes decimated
scattered
yet still blooming in pockets

like hidden forest flowers

*

But history has taught her
to be inscrutable –
this Cassava-Mama

Grating into her Amazon-basin.
So watch her closely
and read between the lines –

The way she
squeezes
her matapee

The way she puts
her cassava-bread
moons to dry

The way she sifts
like any pork-knocker
a river's residue
from the hard gold of her life

*

But if she should turn
her rain-forest eyes

Beckoning me

into an Amerindian
pre-history

Would I take my courage
in both hands and go –
Through the dark

Door-mouth of forest
past that Olmec head
massive and enigmatic

Past the veil of secrecy
where the old Gods await me –
the glittering fragments and bones?

*

So many forgotten gods and tribes
So many hardened ritual sites –
the skeletons of so many stories
all waiting to be re-fleshed by me
all waiting to be awakened with a kiss
like sleeping beauty.

*

But don't imagine that I Cariwoma
hanker after some lost El Dorado
or yearn for the flowers
of a blood-shedding mythology –
An obsidian dagger in a captive heart.
Atahualpa's grim mantle.
Montezuma's long shadow.

Lianas of time pushed back
to find myself a path
                    a map
Or better yet some dappled
forest clearing
to sit and contemplate
the vastness of this dreaming

So that Moon would continue
in its sailing openness

So that Sun would rise up each day
full and replenished

So that Stars would not lose hold
of their gold

So that Moon in fit of jealousy
would not swallow Sun

So that Sun in greedy turn
would not eat-up moon

So that Stars would not put
each other's eyes to the spear

So that Sun, Moon, Stars would not
suddenly vanish

So that the earth would not be plunged
into everlasting darkness – for this

43

Many an Aztec eye endured
the accumulation of skulls in the plazas

The blood-carpeted steps of the temple.

The prophetic texts
of the Mayan priests
long sequestered
among stones

The ancient ones who rose up
with swimming faces
and glazed eyes
to speak of the coming anguish

The humiliation of:
the featherless quetzal
the clawless eagle
the toothless jaguar

Gold was their goal
And gold was their God
Gold was their love
And gold was their song
Gold was their thirst
and gold was their hunger
Such golden obsessions
Could only create golden monsters

A king who dusted himself in gold dust each day
before rinsing himself in a gold-silted lake.
A land whose mossy rocks were really
(you guessed it) ingots of pure gold
amber rivers rushing – not towards their own destines
but glistening with the flakes of El Dorado

And whenever they turned towards us
always that conquistadorial yearning
always the same burning question
from their gold-smiting mouths –
'The gold in your ears and nose
where did you get it from?
where did you get it from?'

The history books were right
about one thing – we did die like flies.
What they didn't mention was
the mumbled way we cursed ourselves
even as the cord of death tightened
around our breath – we cursed ourselves
more than we cursed them –
for the 'Taino' that came so easy to our lips.
How we still yearn after so many moons
to fight it out in the green arena
skin grating skin like iguanas
without the thunder of those hooves
the cowardice of the canon.

The parrots that mocked us
also mocked them

Their green laughter
Their raucous words

Sucked like shadows
into the invisible kingdom
where all words go.

Quetzalcoatl
comes sailing to my door
on his raft of snakes

Bringing with him
the gift
of three birds –

The Quetzal
The Continga
And the Roseate Spoonbill

How he rides me –
This Lord of Wisdom
and all abilities

His headdress – a riotous waterfall
shielding my eyes
from the flame of his face

Gently blowing
all of Meso-America
through the flute of my ears.

How can there be a heaven without Xocolatl
wondrous beverage from the tree Cacahuaquchtl?

O pass me the cup –
Let me drink of
the smooth and bitter brew
sweetened with honey and chillies –
Your gift, Quetzalcoatl, of El Dorado darkness

You who shimmer before me now
No longer Plumed-Saviour
or Feathered-Serpent
No longer Lord of the Dawn
or Lord of the Four Winds –
Just my own returning melting Chocolate-God

If there is a heaven without Xocolatl
I'll give that paradise a miss
O divine bearer of the cacoa-pod.

And why shouldn't I let myself
be possessed by the gods?
Why shouldn't I open myself
to their amorous advances?
They who never think
that a woman is past it –
they for whom whiling
away some time with a mortal
is but a drop in eternity's ocean.

Zeus, Zeus,
whatever happen between us
is we business.

Keeper of the green cathedral –

Ceiling of high foliage,
mossy mosaic groundwork,
heartland pillars rising
insistent as bird-choiring.

And suddenly from behind a dark vestry –
the old deer-footed leaf-bearded
curator himself, Papa Bois,
emerging with his familiar
squelch and crackle.

Craggy face lit by a stained
forest-window of light,
pausing beside a waterfall –
his altar-place of misty communion.

Listen to the stirrings of his vast
half-hidden congregation.

Four

The one whose forehead
underwent a crisis
in that metropolis –
still fine and smooth but cast
with the shadowing imprint.
A crisis of papers unfixed,
two three jobs as domestic
and weathering the cold,
the barrel in her kitchen-corner
a ship's hold, constantly
waiting to be filled –

This time with bargain clothes,
employers' cast-offs
for the children back home.
The children all waiting for her
to find a survival-kit
that would lead to citizenship
(a few Anansi tricks)
Waiting for her to clear
a sky of fog, a path of snow,
so that they could follow.

Boy going to join his mother in Canada
study bad. Turn lawyer.
Girl taking the flower of herself elsewhere.
Turn nurse. Maybe doctor.
Whole families sucked abroad.

Through the glass of the departure lounge
old canecutter watches it all
face a study of diasporic brooding.
Watches the silver shark
waiting on the tarmac.

Watches until the shuddering monster
takes off with his one
and only grandson –
leaving behind a gaping hole
in the glittering sea we call sky.

But now outside the airport building
where emotions are no longer checked in,
the old man surrenders
to his gut-instinct,
sinking to his knees on the grass.

His cane-shot eyes
his voice cracked as he wails
what his bones know for certain:
'*Nevaar* to meet again
Nevaar to meet again'

Come, Hanuman,
only your many arms
can help console this man –
still waving to an empty sky
the white flag of his handkerchief.

Who knows why they leave
racing like lemmings into the blue beyond?

It is more than the sun-limitation
or the moneyless horizon

More than the political confusion
or call of innermost vocation

Perhaps the truth lies with the birds that fly
over the heads of immigration officers

Mi dear, times hard
but things lush-lush here
on this piece of stream
of conscious landscape –
this wilful Eden trod on by every race.

You see this tree here with its fine
filigree of leaves? That is Tamarind.
The little pods sour like sour
but roll Tamarind in brown sugar
and you long to put it in your mouth.

This one here, wearing her fruits
like rosy drop-pearl earrings,
answer to the name of Spice Mango.
You staring at the Queen of Fruit Trees.
For sweetness and poise you can't beat she.

Growing down there like a green chandelier
is the one pretending to be a tree.
Yet I call that little sucker, the Tree-of-Life,
for Banana can feed the planet,
each finger a little meal-in-a-jacket.

Mind you don't mash my pumpkin vine,
but if you look up to the sky
you'll see the orbs and sceptres
of the Coconut Tree. You can tell
that one is related to royalty.

Waving breezy in the field over there
like he got short memory,
is of course Sugarcane.
But his history so long, mi dear,
I saving him for another day.

Yes, through it all
Cane still dancing
green in sun and breeze
still glistening and rippling –
No matter how we
burn and chop him
no matter how we
crush and boil him
no matter how we
curse and blame him –
Next year he up again
hands in the air
waving fresh-fresh as ever
a carefree carnival character –
Mr Midas, the man
with the golden touch
or better yet
original alchemist
spilling his crystal-seed
his tiny jewels
of transformation
at our weeping feet.

Resting my face against
the soft flames of your petals
breathing in your subtle
almost no-smelling fragrance
touching your stigma, stamen, pollen,
touching your dark green
serrated leaves that gently support
your inexpressible beauty
your unquenchable thirst for sun and rain.

Hibiscus – everywhere
red, open and not without sorrow
like your people.

From the fortress of its buttress
right up to its wide
spreading branches
Silk Cotton Tree
breathes standoffishness –

Not the kind of tree, my friend,
to threaten with an axe.
They say canoe hacked from its trunk
bound to meet a sticky end.
Not the kind of tree to gather round
for test match post-mortem
or hang about aimless and boldface
like those young men
mouthing their soft obscenities
under its wounded shade –
testing, I tell you, the patience of legend.

Hug-me-Close
Search-me-Heart and Sweetsop
Neem Bush
Bitter Bush and Strongback
Baby-Gripe
Teasam and Carilla
Sweetbroom
Mint and Sarsparilla

Lemon-Grass
Zeb-Grass and Vervine
Congo-Pump
Mini-Root and Sea-time
Leaf-of-Life
Womb-Weed and Semen-Contra
White-Sage
Madam-Faith and John-de-Conqueror

Sly Anansi know how to tease me,
like that time he sense

My second-thoughts shift
about the propriety of our tryst.

Hear he, fingers
moonlighting on my knee;

'Woman shouldn't think you know,
Woman should just act.

Too much thinking-thinking
can lead to dry river valley,

Woman is nature and nature is power.
Eh! Eh! When nature shrug we run fuh cover.

No, thinking does not lead
to peak-experience ecstasy.'

Hmmm . . .
I thinking all the same

How I can use weave of words
To bend web of laws,

How I can submit papers,
inserting clause –

In other words, how I can make
full claim on cyclone, storm, hurricane –

And every eddy eddying forth
from my warm unstable edges.

Yes, how I can keep clear conscience
while easing the low pressures

Rising natural-natural
from my interfrontal zone.

Five

You there, Hummingbird,
my iridescent messenger –
What news now, what revelation,
you pollinating-child-of-the-sun?

The sleep-inducing rain
beating down on the galvanise
is just iron-man Ogun
turning his hand to steelpan

The clatter of wind in the trees
is just Oya scattering her vocals
among an acoustics of leaves

The rolling and receding thunder
is just Shango hitting his old drum-kit
with some new lightning-riffs.

It was at a coastal-do
I came across you, Kali,
locked in the karmic-dance
of your combatant-spirit

Head swinging –
a frantic pendulum
from the column
of your own body-clock

Feet
earth-rooted
Shiva your
recumbent rock

And every singeing swing
of your hair's unruly wind –
a tribute to the dead
a reminder to the living

Here the sacrificial goat
Here the bed of burning coals
Here the dark awakening
Here the bright threshold

The way the red sun surrenders

its wholeness to curving ocean

bit by bit. The way curving ocean

gives birth to the birth of stars

in the growing darkness,

wearing everything in its path

to cosmic smoothness.

The impulse of stones rolling

towards their own roundness.

The unexpected comets of flying fish.

And Forest, Great-Breathing-Spirit,
rooting to the very end –
for the life of this planet.

Bathing in the misty cauldron of Sea
with the plain sky above my head
and the grit of smooth sand under my feet –
I face up to blue exultant waters
and the little houses clinging
to the hillside in the distance –
the hutches of the poor whose ancestors
including mine – worked the hot labourious fields –

For them I bask
a kind of ancestral back-pay.

Follow that painting back –
the long forgotten one
still gracing the Big House wall.
The gilded frame; the tones and shades;
old gold and browns –
Just who is this autumnal English gentleman?
This baccra-ancestor –
His pastoral-pose now abandoned to plantation ghosts.

By all means note with care –
The dead hare lying at his feet;
The cobwebbed-symmetry of his hunting gun
and good dog looking up – knowing its place
in empire's scheme of things.

And further back behind those Elizabethan curtains;
Our own unframed drama of flames and whips –
An oldworld-newworld saga of loss and pillage.
And though I Cariwoma prefer not to dwell
on the wrongs of history, I must bear witness –
To the invisible frieze of lips.
To sculptural hurts which I must try to heal
if only with my balm of words.

Chile, I won't put
my head on a block
or make guesswork
about anyone's ancestry.

Our shades of kin.
Our colour-schemes
do range from ebony
to ivory.

Yes, I too am out-foxed
and flummoxed
by the mingling flesh
of history's passions –

Like that black calypsonian
singing bewilderedly;
'Chinee children
calling me daddy.'

And is so mouth open
and story jump out
And is so blood weave tapestry
from scandal in family.

Their letters come few
And far between

Ex-cursions of ghosts
In envelopes of absence?

Yet in them I savour
The scent of oak trees

The golden plaitedness
Of wheat

Before old winter takes over.
The stoic blackbird

Picking its way once more
Along the sandy snowy fields.

No ceilings of stone cherubs and seraphs –

Yet I have seen angels dangling
casual legs from the leafy
architecture in my backyard.
Those spacious green domes
that shield from sun.
Secrets whispered to palm trees
tolerant columns –
For me an everyday renaissance.

(for Lesley)

How good to see the sunshine
still in your eyes –
my come-home-to-visit daughter.
How good to know that the cold
hasn't put on you – a dampener.

Your arms still bringing gift-hugs.
Your face hanging like a lamp
onto my every story-telling word.

Surely for you, Moon-Gazer will turn up
once more outside your window?
Surely for you, Mama-Wata
will make her subtle
splash more audible?
And everywhere flowers will re-bloom
their names on your memory.

Many have stamped themselves
with the ink of exile.

But you, my daughter
from a land of many waters –
belong to the world.

The children of Las Margaritas
in the State of Chiapas are dancing,
but who are they honouring,
hands raised towards the heavens?
Is it the rain-god, Tlaloc?
Is it Mary or Jesus?
Is it the goddess of the ripening
maize, Chicomecoatl?

Like their ancestors before them,
who have themselves become deities
through their suffering and dying –
the children of Las Margaritas
in the State of Chiapas are dancing;
have entered the dance.

They are dancing for freedom, for bright
Quetzal colours.
They are dancing for justice, recompense
for old and new violations.
They are dancing for themselves,
here, on this plateau, with the rains
drifting down from the mountains.

Through the grounding of the yellow corn
and the grounding of the white corn
Through the mixing and the moulding
of the maize with the water
Flesh-of-corn
Blood-of-water
They were born

Jaguar Quitze
Jaguar Night
Mahucutah
True Jaguar
(These were the first men)

Celebrated Seahouse
Prawn House
Hummingbird House
Macaw House
(These were the first women)

The great ladies, as they say, who
together with the first men, gave birth
to all the tribes.

The first people of the Quiche Maya
fashioned by the Bearer-Begetter
Maker-Modeler

Walking and wondering
Talking and praising
giving thanks – double thanks
triple thanks.

As if I'd eaten labba
and drunk the proverbial creek water

As if I'd been seduced
by the lure of the Cascadura

As if I'd made a covenant
something keeps me to these shores –

Here where trade winds breathe islands
and scarlet ibises sear the horizon
and faces startle with their sudden
cheek-bones of survival.

Sea right here on your lipshore
is where I Cariwoma must come
to reacquaint with all of me.
Right here on your shifting sands
is where I must face up
to life's cosmic exclamations.
So come Sea, make we catch up
on all the labrish since you last see me –
Let me hear once more your mouthwash
echoes in my own voicespeak.

Today I sing of Sea self
a glittering breathing
in a turquoise dress

Constantly stitched and re-stitched
by the bright seamstresses of flying-fish
adding a thousand sapphire touches

With no boat or ship to darken
the hem of her horizon
no shadows cast

Just the straight rising sun
Sea memory is as clear
as a desert island

And I am on the edge
of this new world
awaiting the footprints of my arrival

Glossary

Anansi   Mythical shape-shifting spider of West African cosmology and the wily trickster figure of West Indian Anancy folktales.

Atahualpa   The Inca ruler at the time of Pizarro's invasion of Peru. Regarded with fear and awe by his people as a direct descendant of the sun.

Baccra   Creole term for a white person.

Cacahuaquchtl Mayan name for the cacao tree.

Cascadura   There is a Trinidadian belief that those who eat of the Cascadura fish will be destined to return to Trinidad.

Cassandra	Prophetess in Greek mythology who spoke the truth but fated never to be believed.
Cassava	The root-vegetable, manioc.
Chachalaka	Bird hunted and domesticated by the Indians.
Chicomecoatl	Mexican corn goddess
Duenne	Spirit of unbaptised child that wanders the forest goblin-like with feet turned backwards.
El Dorado	Fabled city of gold that lured European explorers to the rivers and mountains of South America during the sixteenth and early seventeenth centuries. Rumours of this wealthy kingdom based on the Golden Man (El Hombre Dorado) – a magnificent king who would wash gold dust from his skin in the middle of a lake.
Guanahani	(San Salvador), *Liamuiga* (St Kitts), *Wa-omoni* (Barbuda), *Kairi* (Trinidad), *Kiskeya* (Dominican Republic), *Alliouagana*

(Montserrat), *Madinina* (Martinique),
Xaymaca (Jamaica), *Iounalao* (St Lucia) –
original Amerindian names of these
Caribbean islands.

Hanuman   Loyal monkey god of Hindu mythology.

Intihuatana   Stone pillar, a type of sundial found at
Macchu Picchu. The word itself means
'Hitching post for the sun'. It was the
place to which the priests tied the sun at
the point of its furthest distance from the
southern hemisphere (winter solstice) so
that it would begin to come back again.

Kali   Hindu goddess with her necklace of
skulls, identified both with destruction
and dynamic energy.

Labba   There is a Guyanese belief that those
who eat of the wild meat labba and
drink creekwater will return to end their
days in Guyana.

Macchu Picchu Fortified city, high above the
Urubamba River. A ruined complex of
terraces, gabled houses and sacred

plazas carved out in the Andes that bear witness to Inca architecture.

Malinche   Amerindian woman who was the translator for Hernan Cortes during the Spanish Conquest of 1521. She bore him a son who is seen symbolically as the first *mestizo*, a child of mixed race. *Malinchista* later became an insulting expression for betrayal.

Mama-Wata   West African mermaid-figure whose Caribbean sister is also known as Fair Maid or Water-Mama.

Montezuma   Aztec Emperor who bestowed gifts on the conquistadores in the hope that the strangers would leave. He believed the Spanish Cortes to be a reincarnation of the exiled Quetzalcoatl, a culture hero and Lord of the Dawn.

Moon-Gazer   Supernaturally-tall folk figure who straddles the crossroads gazing at the moon.

Ogun	God of iron in the Yoruba pantheon. Related to the steel-drum through his identification with metal.
Oya	Yoruba goddess of the winds and tornadoes. She represents sweeping change.
Papa Bois	A Pan-like cloven-foot father-protector of the forest and its creature inhabitants.
Penelope	Wife of Odysseus who remained true to him during his long absence. She was besieged with suitors who had moved into the palace. Penelope had promised to choose one of them as king when she was finished weaving a tapestry. But what she wove by day she unravelled by night.
Persephone	Daughter of Zeus and Demeter (agricultural goddess) who was snatched by Hades to the underworld. Through the pleas of her mother to the other gods she was allowed back each year (spring and summer).

Popocatepetl and *Iztaccihuatl*   Twin volcanoes looming
above Mexico city. Their names mean-
ing 'Smoking Mountain' and 'White
Lady'.

Pork-knocker   Prospector for gold or diamonds in the
rivers of the Guyana hinterland. Salted
pork, a regular part of their diet, hence
the nickname.

Quetzal   Feathers of the Quetzal bird, like jade,
were precious to the Aztecs.

Quetzalcoatl   The Toltec god/king, the Plumed
Serpent who brought the gift of learning
and the seeds of the divine chocolate-
giving cacao.

Shango   Yoruba god of thunder and lightning.

Silk-Cotton Tree   Also known as the Ceiba and Kapok
tree. An enormous tree that grows both
in Africa and the Caribbean. Said to
attract ancestral spirits and linked to a
number of superstitions.

Taino   Arawak speaking tribe of the Caribbean.
The word also means peace..

Tenochtitlan   Original Mexican capital whose splendour greatly impressed the Spanish conquistadors.

Tlaloc   Aztec rain god.

Wapishana/Macusi/Warrau   Names of some of the Amerindian tribes in Guyana.

Xocolatl   Special drink made from the beans of the cacao which was both a food and a form of currency.

Zeus   Head of the Olympian Gods after he dethroned his father, Cronus.